Stuck? : When Your Dream Becomes Work

By Chloe Hill

ST IVES MEDIA

First published in Australia in 2016
By St Ives Media
stivesmedia.com.au

St Ives Media
P.O. Box 52
Nunawading VIC 3131,
Australia

National Library of Australia Cataloguing-in-Publication data: (pending)

Hill, Chloe
          Stuck? : When Your Dream Becomes Work / Chloe Hill
          ISBN: 978-0-9922675-8-2 (paperback)
          ISBN: 978-0-9922675-9-9 (ebook)
          Quality of work life
          Self-realization
          Self-actualization (Psychology)
          Quality of life
          St Ives Media
650.1

Cover design by: St Ives Media
Internal design and graphics by: St Ives Media

This book is dedicated to
all of you attempting to live your dreams;
You are not alone

INTRODUCTION

"The only thing worse than not getting what you want is getting what you want" - OSCAR WILDE

Many of us have become inspired at a point in our lives to strike out for something new. Often we have to hear this siren call several times before we're really motivated to act on it, but then we do. We quit our jobs, become entrepreneurs, write for a living or set off on some other crazy sounding adventure that takes us down the 'road less travelled'.

Everything's awesome in the beginning!

We're patting ourselves on the back for our courage and we're the envy of all our friends. But then we have to get down to it, and start actually delivering on all our talk. This is when we begin to find that what started with so much courage is now a lot harder than we thought. As the first flush of enthusiasm starts to wear thin, we shrivel down into ourselves and become STUCK.

So, we gather more 'wisdom' - quotes, mantras, inspirational podcasts and courses etc., but still feel like we're drowning in information that never seems quite enough. The momentum runs out, as we spiral into self-doubt and start to feel like failures. This is the point were many people are tempted to give up and do; then spend the rest of their lives regretting what might have been.

This book is about forging a path through these inevitable hurdles. It's about what to do when you've jumped and sure, the net has appeared, but it's feeling pretty flimsy at best!

Written primarily for people starting a new business or artistic endeavour, the ideas and principles could as easily be applied to anything large or scary you've set out to do.

Read from cover to cover or just dip into the parts that sound most relevant - whatever works best for you. Hopefully it'll provide you with ideas and support to get you unstuck and moving forward.

Cheers ☺

Chloe

Chapter 1 - GENERAL STUFF TO THINK ABOUT

"Leap and the net will appear" – *JOHN BURROUGHS*

Kanter's Law: "Everything looks like a failure in the middle" – *ROSABETH MOSS KANTER*

"I don't really believe in writer's block, but I absolutely believe in getting stuck" – *NEIL GAIMAN*

Transition Period

Congratulations! You've just made a significant life change and are now in a state of Transition.

Transitions always involve uncertainty and change, even when you have a destination clearly in mind. Our individual responses to transitions vary depending on our personalities and life experience. For most people, regardless of temperament, periods of transition last longer than expected.

It's easy to underestimate the enormity of this adjustment phase. It impacts your orientation to the world, the people you hang out with and your values and beliefs. The key thing to remember is that if you're doing it 'right' it should feel uncomfortable as you're exposed to new experiences.

You may be someone who didn't previously know anyone who was living a less than conventional life. So you're still essentially immersed in the world you've come from. You may have also stirred up other people's envy as they begin see your actions as a direct criticism of their own inertia. No one likes to feel lonely and we all want to belong. So the temptation is to continue hanging out with the types of people you've always hung out with, but as you change so must your world. It's hard in the beginning to step away from what is comfortable and into uncertainty. If you continue to stay in your familiar milieu, measuring yourself against old yardsticks and ways of doing things, you'll fall prey to your fears and lose momentum. This is particularly important when you're in the process of forging a new identity.

Finding a new 'tribe' of people with whom your changed or emerging values are more aligned may not be that straightforward, depending on where you live. These fellow travellers are just as likely to be people you don't yet know exist, or they may be people who you're meeting for the first time, so you don't yet have much depth of connection with them.

Even people who appear to have their act together and seem well connected are grappling with the same issues as you. They feel like loners at times, voices in the wilderness and are trying to find their own tribes. They're in a constant process of building and strengthening their people networks for success and you need to do the same.

The Change Curve

The Kubler-Ross Change Curve was originally developed to describe a person's grief response to the death of an intimate partner. It has subsequently been used to illustrate adaption to change more generally.

People spend differing amounts of time in each stage of the curve. EVERYONE has a point at which they find change hard or areas of their life where it's more confronting, regardless of the level of optimism they may have displayed in the beginning.

Fig 1 - The Kubler-Ross Change Curve

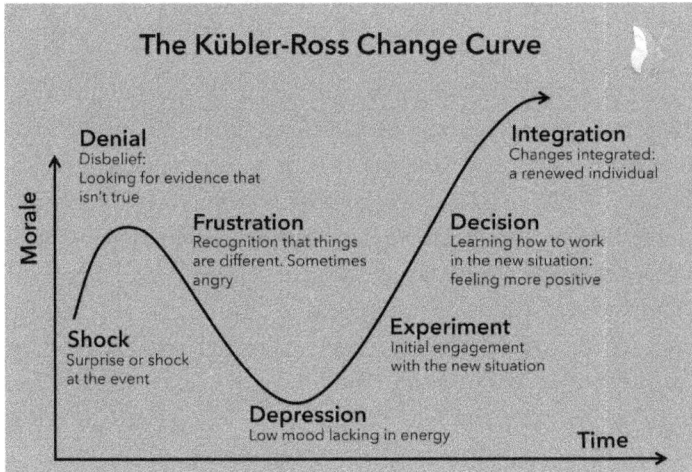

The key stages are:

- ✓ **Shock** - surprise or shock at the event
- ✓ **Denial** - disbelief, looking for evidence that it isn't true

- ✓ **Frustration** - recognition that things are different; sometimes angry
- ✓ **Depression** - low mood; lacking in energy
- ✓ **Experiment** - initial engagement with the new situation
- ✓ **Decision** - learning how to work in the new situation; feeling more positive
- ✓ **Integration** - changes integrated; a renewed individual

The significant element to note here is TIME. What seems impossible now will moderate over time, as your morale and competence improves.

What people don't always fully appreciate is that these stages apply, whether you've initiated the change or whether it's been thrust on you. If you've picked up this book, your state of mind is probably located somewhere between Frustration, Depression and Experiment. You may cycle through these different stages many times, spending more time in some and a lot less in others. You will also have periods where you think you're completely transitioned, only to have a negative experience and revert back. The range of what is considered normal response is broad.

The key thing to remember is that as you transition through these different stages, your sense of being overwhelmed, frustrated, angry or depressed will diminish as your feelings of competency increase. Even when you're familiar with this model, you can become so caught up in the immediacy of your circumstances, you lose your perspective and no longer appreciate that what you are experiencing is simply an emotional reaction to change. The key task remains the same however, which is to take where you've been and where you want to go and integrate those selves into a stronger whole.

As a society, we're strongly encouraged to deny or suppress our more negative emotional responses. Consequently we often don't possess the vocabulary or experience to manage these emotions within ourselves. As much as you may want to accentuate the positive, it's counterproductive if it comes at the expense of denying your more negative emotions. This stuff it can be hard to talk about, while you're still grappling with it yourself.

When you made the decision to embark on this new direction you were in receipt of only so much information that you viewed through a particular lens. Now you have more advanced information, gained through your personal experience, you're seeing the world differently; don't underestimate the importance of this distinction. It's the critical difference between an idea and a reality.

An important thing to remember is that just because you're going through a rough patch doesn't mean the decision to embark on this new endeavor was the wrong one. It just means you need to take stock and arm yourself with some new skills and mindsets to transition successfully - all it takes is time, the right mentors and information.

Your New 'Normal'

You're now at a point where you've probably got used to a whole new state of 'normal'. Remember the concepts behind Maslow's Hierarchy of Needs?

Fig 2 – Maslow's Hierarchy of Needs

In Maslow's Hierarchy our needs build upon each other. It's only when our more basic requirements are comfortably met that our desire to fulfill additional needs elevates up the pyramid. In your particular case, because you've started on your new direction, you're no longer dealing with your previous frustrations. For example, you're no longer at your old workplace tolerating co-workers and the monotony of your old job. These frustrations that used to preoccupy you daily have receded into the background. Now you're grappling with a different set of imperfect issues and have a new definition of 'normal'.

Consequently it's easy to lose perspective and underestimate the huge adjustments you've already made.

Some approaches

✓ **Acknowledge the transition phase** - Recognise you're in a transition phase that's perfectly legitimate. You don't have to deny or pretend it's not happening, you need to work through it. Don't be afraid to put up the 'Under Construction' sign and accept that all elements of your life can't proceed as if nothing is happening. Recognise you may be undergoing changes to your sense of identity and orientation to the world at this point. You're in the process of pulling apart and rebuilding yourself anew. Be kind to yourself, realise it's ok to wobble. You're not a machine and transitioning through this process is never linear.

✓ **Familarise yourself with the change curve** - This will help you to understand your emotions and state of mind. Being able to put a name to whatever phase you're in will make it more straightforward to understand. It's an individual experience. Whatever works for you is perfectly fine, whether you cycle through these phases hourly, daily or weekly.

✓ **Accept that it always takes longer than you think** - Recalibrate your expectations about the time it takes to adjust to the new.

✓ **Rehearse your spiel** - Start practicing how you now define yourself. This is not just about spin it's about forging your new sense of self. In the beginning, while you're still coming to terms with your own shifting identity, it can be tempting to fudge and deflect attention. Without some rehearsed phrases at the ready, you can come off sounding unconvincing or vague if you feel put on the spot. A short prepared spiel or 'elevator pitch' will help you grow into your new identity and connect with other likeminded people.

Dissect and Take Stock

Now is a good time to create a snapshot of your current situation by dissecting and taking stock.

Nothing is ever all good or bad, and what you usually discover is that you have a few problem areas rather than a wholesale disaster. Teasing out a more granular picture will provide perspective and allow you to identify the best actions you can take.

Assess your mood and emotions

Take a mood check.

Often your strong emotional reaction to a situation can cause you to give it more weight than it truly deserves. We all carry around our baggage. Assessing your emotional areas singularly will identify strengths as well as weaknesses.

Go with your gut response and on a scale of 1-5 - where 1 = Very Poor and 5 = Excellent - assess the state of the following within yourself:

	1	2	3	4	5
General mood					
Accountability					
Resilience					
Confidence					
Optimism					
Resourcefulness					
Relaxation					

Attitude to the future					
Control of anxiety					
Management of fear					
Management of anger					

A guide to the scoring:

Rating of 50+ - Excellent - You're extremely optimistic and sound like you're managing your emotions well.

A word of caution: You could be in denial over some aspects of your personality if your self-knowledge is not as reliable as you may think. This may cause problems down the track if you're not adapting for your weaknesses. (Everybody has them!)

Rating of 40-50 - Very Good - You're on the very optimistic side, but this also seems tempered with a fair degree of realism about yourself.

Rating of 30-40 - Good - You have some problems areas where you're not firing well, but overall your state of mind is healthy. You've done an excellent job of identifying areas that might need further work and now is the perfect time to take the opportunity to rectify them.

Rating of less than 30 - Poor - You've assessed yourself as struggling to cope in all of these emotional areas, which is a cause for serious concern. While all is not lost, there's work to do on a number of fronts and potentially some hard decisions to be made about your choices and lifestyle.

This list of emotions has been structured as building blocks in order of priority. Each emotional state builds on the one before. If you're looking at where to focus your efforts, start from the top and work down. If you make a start by improving your sense of Accountability and Confidence this will flow through to an improvement in your other emotional areas.

Identify your particular fears

Everyone has specific fears that are easily activated, especially when we're under stress. Your changing circumstances may have stirred up fears that you could have spent years, consciously or unconsciously, insulating yourself against.

Your emotional reactions to any of the following (either their presence or absence in your life) could trigger your fear responses:

- ✓ Money
- ✓ Security
- ✓ Status
- ✓ Love
- ✓ Sense of individuality
- ✓ Requests for help
- ✓ Competence
- ✓ Control
- ✓ Being liked

- ✓ Being perfect
- ✓ Being envied
- ✓ Being dominant
- ✓ Be relevant
- ✓ Being a leader
- ✓ Being told what to do

Make a note of the fears, which resonate with you from this list or others you've identified.

Pick your greatest fear and write down four things:

- ✓ The name of your fear
- ✓ Why you fear this thing
- ✓ What is the likelihood of this fear materialising
- ✓ What is the worst thing that could happen

Articulating your greatest fear by spelling it out on paper, will help you see it in perspective, rather than letting it swirl around preoccupying your thoughts.

Celebrate your achievements

List ten things you've accomplished so far and celebrate them. The list doesn't have to be earth shattering it could be something like:

- ✓ A skill you've mastered
- ✓ A course you've taken
- ✓ Creation of an organised workspace
- ✓ Your first contract negotiation
- ✓ Your first sale
- ✓ Mastery of Twitter
- ✓ Organisation of an travel itinerary
- ✓ Your first public speaking engagement
- ✓ A successful networking lead
- ✓ A spectacular failure that has taught you a lot about something!

The main thing is to acknowledge these accomplishments and celebrate them in some way. You've come further than you think, and celebrating your achievements will help you to appreciate your very real progress.

Pat yourself on the back, open a bottle of champagne or treat yourself in some other meaningful way.

What have you learned?

Hint: It's more than you think

Next: Think about what you've learned over this time.

Focusing on what you've learned is different to focusing on your accomplishments. Here, I want you to make a warts and all assessment about what you've learned about yourself over past weeks or months so you can use this information to identify areas for potential improvement.

These are the types of questions to ask yourself:

✓ What have you learned about the degree of difficulty – Are things harder than you thought?

✓ What have you learned about your motivation?

✓ What have you learned about the concept of freedom – Are you discovering the paradox of too much freedom?

✓ Are certain things easier than you thought?

✓ Are dormant skills coming valuably to the fore?

✓ Are you at sea without proper routines to your days and weeks?

✓ Do you use your time better or worse than you imagined?

✓ Have you surprised yourself in some way?

What is the next action you can take?

There's always an action step you can take in any situation to continue moving forward. This next step doesn't have to be big, it just has to be an action step you can take, that isn't just a form of escape or denial.

For example, can you do one of the following today:

- ✓ Send an email
- ✓ Write one more sentence for your novel
- ✓ Phone one person who may be a valuable contact
- ✓ Take a walk to lift your mood or stimulate new ideas
- ✓ Update your website
- ✓ Organise a Meetup in your area
- ✓ Develop some promotional ideas
- ✓ Write and email to someone who is already a practitioner in the field you want to move into asking for their help
- ✓ Generate one new idea
- ✓ Tidy up or throw something out
- ✓ Dedicate time to something important

The list is really endless, but the important thing is that you see yourself as empowered to chart your own way. Do something that moves your situation forward and then tomorrow do one more thing.

Chapter 2 - COMMON CHALLENGES - and How to Manage Them

"Whether you think you can, or think you can't – you're right" – *HENRY FORD*

"The bad news is you're falling through the air, nothing to hang on to, no parachute. The good news is there's no ground" – *CHOYAM TRUNGPA RINPOCHE*

"If you spend 4 hours a day on anything, you're going to become pretty good, even if you have zero talent"

- ROBERT RODRIGUEZ

In the previous chapter you were asked to create a snapshot of your current situation by:

- ✓ Acknowledging your state of transition
- ✓ Assessing your mood and emotions
- ✓ Taking stock of what you have learned, your fears and accomplishments
- ✓ Taking the logical next step

In this section we want to focus on the common challenges that can derail you. There will be some overlap, especially when it comes to addressing the problem, a single solution may address a number of challenges at once.

Fear / Self-Doubt

This is the 'mother' of all issues.

Unfortunately, fear and self-doubt will be your frequent companions if you're striking out to do something new and big for the first time. Even the most confidant and seemingly together people are scared at times. It's just not something people talk about openly and if they do, it's only with those extremely close to them.

There are no grown-ups somewhere with all the answers. There are just more people like yourself with greater or lesser degrees of skills and experience; once you appreciate this truth it can be liberating. We all become brilliant at projecting a competent veneer. There's no 'set and forget' technique that completely bypasses fear.

Instead, focus your efforts on getting more comfortable with an increased tolerance of fear so that it becomes your new normal. This is about focusing your efforts on greater exposure and desensitisation, rather than avoidance.

Learning to embrace fear, failure and potential setbacks is all about expanding your comfort zone as you transition into a more confident and capable person. Facing your fears head on takes the wind out of its sails and can make you feel as if you can kick ass! You'll become excited about what more you can achieve.

Some approaches

✓ **Embrace fear and self-doubt** - Realise that fear and self-doubt are signs you're operating outside your comfort zone because you're learning. See them as positives and a necessary part of the process. Rather like breaking eggs to make omelets.

✓ **Your self worth is not always on the line** - Learn to separate your feelings of uncertainty about something new from your general feelings of self-worth. Just because something didn't work out doesn't mean you're a failure. It just means you experimented and now know more than you did before.

✓ **Suspend your negative self-talk** - Become more conscious of the amount of damaging self-talk you subject yourself to on a regular basis. Try a technique used in Cognitive Behavourial Therapy (CBT). At the first sign of a negative thought you shove it immediately through a trapdoor under the floor or throw it out the window; whatever mental image works best for you. The main thing is to disarm the flow of negative self-talk by stopping it in its tracks. Your fear response is caused by the speed with which your brain sends signals to the adrenaline producing centers of the body, preparing you for fight or flight, before you've consciously registered what is happening. That's why you feel as if your fears and anxieties seem to come out of nowhere.

✓ **Develop your support team** - Surround yourself with people who believe in you and who provide the support and encouragement you need to thrive. When you're feeling most vulnerable, you may also want to be more selective about who you open up to in the early stages. You don't need your fears unnecessarily stirred up by people who behave mean spiritedly. Don't set yourself up to be a victim by feeling you have to always tell all.

✓ **Practice a form of desensitisation** - Use exposure, rather than avoidance, to gain confidence in reducing these fears rather than letting them limit and control you. While this approach seems counterproductive, it's actually a powerful technique. When you face your fears you effectively neutralise them. Every fear you face will make you grow in confidence. Using techniques such as Rejection Therapy[1] will turn this into a game for you.

✓ **Use your fear to connect with others** - When you reveal the things about yourself you struggle to hide, that's often when you form the most genuine connections with other people. Articulating the truths inside you and getting them out into the daylight is the cornerstone of creating great art. Use your fear as a mechanism to open up conversations and allow yourself to be vulnerable to situations and people. In the beginning just be selective with whom you share.

✓ **Act like a confident person and own it** - When you're doing something new for the first time and don't know what you are doing, act like someone who does. You will then become that person. Never given a public speech before? Act like someone who can give great speeches. Never written a marketing plan? Act like a person who writes marketing plans. Another strategy you can use is to take a person you admire and in situations ask yourself: What would X do? How would they handle this? I remember when I worked in a project a number of years ago and Alan Greenspan was the Chairman of the Federal Reserve in the United

States. We had a refrain in the project: Does Alan Greenspan need to know about this? Would Alan Greenspan attend this meeting? Which was a jokey short hand way of saying: was this important enough to warrant anyone's attention.

Financial Worries

Financial worries can be very real. If you've taken a gamble, it can be as big a problem as your self-doubt and just as paralysing. Most people generally find, when they embark on a new business or creative work, that it takes longer than expected for the activity to become financially viable.

Financial worries can manifest themselves in a number of different ways. They can be centered on your attitudes to money, your skills with finance or how you approach charging for your services.

Many people discover they're not as money or business minded as they thought and they simply lack the financial nous or hustling skills to be successful. This can be particularly challenging for people in the Arts.

You may also discover you're someone who's *way more* anxious about money and financial security than you realised. For peace of mind, you need the reliability of a steady income and a buffer of savings in the bank to function well.

Or you may discover you have deep-seated issues about charging sufficiently for your services. These money blocks can lead you to severely undercharge or give away too much because you struggle to put a real value on what you have to offer.

Whatever the reasons for your financial concerns, learn to take control of the situation, by developing a mechanism to identify areas where you either need to acquire more skills or would be better advised to outsource.

Some approaches

- ✓ **Take a realistic inventory of your current financial situation** - Make the distinction between the following buckets of money:

  - o The amount you currently have to cover your daily, weekly, monthly living expenses
  - o The amount you need to charge for your new services
  - o The cost of providing those services
  - o The money you may need longer term (e.g. insurances)
  - o Current and pipeline income sources

  This exercise is about helping you identify where to focus, by arriving at a realistic assessment of your current financial position. For example, you may have enough in the bank to fund the next six months with a few changes. Or you may identify that your operation cannot viably scale, over the next three months, with your current client list and price structure.

- ✓ **Get financial advice if necessary** - Don't be afraid to get some advice. Maybe you need more information about budgeting, business or even promoting and marketing your services.

- ✓ **Invest in yourself** - Don't be afraid to invest in yourself to develop new skills or identify new sources of information.

- ✓ **Remember you're learning** - If you have underestimated how much time this new venture is going to take, and have simply not set up your finances properly, treat this as another learning experience. Remember that if it were easy, everyone would be doing it. Potentially it's your expectations that need to be reframed.

✓ **Assess your self-esteem around money issues** - There are many good articles, books and websites available on the concept of 'Money Blocks'. Refuse to sell yourself short. Remember when selling services to others that most people are cheap because they either don't think they have the money to be otherwise or like to drive a bargain. It's not about you and the value you bring. Be careful with customers and clients who are high maintenance and difficult, have clear reasons why you're persisting with them. Don't do it just for the money; you'll end up resenting them and the situation.

✓ **Use proper written agreements or contracts for payment** - Make sure you set up proper contracts or agreements **in writing** so that you have a clear mechanism by which you get paid for the work you do. Be direct and commercial in your approach to payments and beware of getting yourself caught up in vague amateur agreements. This can be challenging when you're either charging your friends and family, or dealing with people who are establishing their own start-ups, who may themselves be relatively new to payment processes. It's highly recommended to request at least one upfront payment, so your clients also have some skin in the game.

✓ **Consider alternative sources of income** – If you decide you need to take on some part time or short-term work, just to consolidate your financial position, consider this decision a step on the path to a recommitment of purpose rather than an admission of 'failure'. Think about your best options for both the long and the short term.

✓ **Learn to be more creative with resources like money** - If you've been used to a certain level of income in the past, you may not be someone who is creative about the way you spend money. You may be in the habit of always paying full price without question. Investigate cheaper or alternative options such as exchanges and bartering for services or potentially, not consuming some items at all. There are a lot of advertising pressures bombarding us to spend money to fulfill needs and fears. Be conscious of the 'Why?' around the money you're spending.

Lack of Clear Purpose

A clear sense of purpose or a 'Why' helps you stay motivated and able to prioritise your activities. Without a clear sense of purpose, all manner of distractions and busyness can take hold. You can feel as if you're working really hard, but you're not getting closer to your main goals, because you're mired in activities that are the distracting equivalent of housework.

You don't necessarily need to have an amazing 'solve world hunger' scale of quest, but you do need to have an overarching purpose or focus that's meaningful to *you*.

You probably fall into one of the following categories -

Your purpose is basically sound but:

- ✓ You've just hit a rough patch

- ✓ You haven't revisited your purpose in a while and have forgotten what it is

- ✓ Your purpose needs a few tweaks to improve it

Your purpose is no longer valid because:

- ✓ You were overly influenced by other people's values, so the path you're travelling is not your own

- ✓ You've changed and your purpose no longer fits or has meaning

- ✓ You didn't think to state a purpose or 'Why' from the outset

Whether you have a clearly stated purpose or not; the important thing is to be honest with yourself when you make your purpose assessment.

Some approaches

✓ **State your 'Why'** - If you haven't articulated a 'Why' up to this point then write one down now. The advantage of stating your intention upfront is that when your project/s go through their inevitable ups and downs, you have a clear purpose with which to reignite your enthusiasm. It makes sense to do this at the beginning, but it's not a showstopper if you treat now as a review point to articulate your goal/s.

✓ **Revisit your 'Why' on a regular basis** - Regularly revisit your reasons for embarking on this endeavour in the first place to maintain your enthusiasm. Set up a reminder system that keeps your 'Why' upfront and center, allowing you to frequently reconnect to it. You can also print it out and display it in your workplace, if you are a more visual person.

✓ **Time to recalibrate?** - Maybe your original purpose needs to be refined or recalibrated with the benefit of experience and more information. Sit somewhere quietly and spell this out for yourself.

✓ **State your 'Why' out loud** - Try saying your 'Why' out loud as you look in the mirror and assess how it feels. Is it something that's genuinely meaningful for you? If you're not excited that speaks volumes. You may feel silly at first, but keep practicing until you are able to articulate your purpose out loud without feeling awkward. You'll find this an energising activity to do on a regular basis.

✓ **Fully commit to your chosen course of action** - Once your purpose it crystalised, fully commit to that course of action. Your priorities will shake down much more clearly. Use your 'Why' as an organising principle. Your purpose leads your project in the same way your head leads your body. When you lift your head up straight, your body falls into alignment and you move forward more confidently.

Motivation and Procrastination

Lack of motivation or a tendency to procrastinate will be familiar demons for many people.

This is when you fully appreciate that work does expand to fill the time. Often the more time you have, the less you seem to get done. It's confronting being brought face-to-face with the type of person you really are. It's so much easier to externalise and find excuses.

There's an interesting TED Talk on this topic by Mel Robbins called *How to stop screwing yourself over*.[2] In this 20-minute talk she identifies that the reason why people struggle with their motivation is that most of us grow up expecting to be 'motivated' by an external source like a parent or boss. This socialisation is so ingrained, that we often don't understand why we flounder when this explicit form of motivation is absent from our lives. She argues that we need to understand this is how we are programmed, so we can stimulate this motivation in ourselves.

Even the most productive people suffer from procrastination from time to time; so don't beat up on yourself. Understand and accept this side of your personality, then put mechanisms in place to work with it.

Some approaches

- ✓ **Time box your activities** - This will give you the illusion of less time and create a sense of urgency. It's a productive way to both manage tasks that have a tendency to blow out or to absorb time, like addressing your email, and tasks which are a hard slog that you may be tempted to give up on too soon (e.g. writing a blog post or a proposal). For example, so as not to get yourself drawn into extensive time on social media; allow yourself say 10 minutes in which to check your social media sites. Set the timer on your phone and then stick to it. Or give yourself two days or even two hours to write a blog post.

✓ **Create rewards** - Set up rewards for doing difficult tasks using the carrot and stick approach. Maybe at the end of your two hours spent on your blog post, give yourself a reward like checking your social media sites.

✓ **Cycles** - People tend to cycle naturally between periods of productivity and rest. Understanding your cycle, and structuring your activities accordingly, provides the most sustainable approach to long-term effectiveness. Otherwise you fall into the trap of pretending you're a perpetual motion machine that can work to capacity every waking moment. Your body and brain both need 'goof off' time to relax, otherwise you create a recipe for burnout.

✓ **Plan** - Create a realistic plan and stick to it. People grossly overestimate what they can achieve in a day and underestimate what can be achieved in a year. Get rid of your crazy, ever lengthening 'To Do' list. Distil activities down to one key outcome that you're going to complete that day.

✓ **Routines** - Set up routines for regular activities, so they don't overload your mental space and become burdensome. For example, pay invoices once a week at a set time or check in with your email only once or twice a day. You don't then need to think about these activities at other times because you have set up regular mechanisms to address them.

Lack of Skills and Experience

Children are learning new things all the time, but as adults we get out of the habit. We reach a point where we no longer regularly put ourselves into learning situations. Unfortunately for many people, this feeling of being a novice stirs up uncomfortable emotions around vulnerability and powerlessness. We insulate ourselves even further from new experiences and opt to play it safe. In our minds, being an 'adult' means *always* demonstrating mastery of our world, but the big risk here is that we stultify and stop growing.

The realisation that you lack important skills, or that the skills you have are not as strong or as competitive as you thought, taps into these feeling of vulnerability. Many studies done on learning methods show that when you start gaining more knowledge on a topic, you'll always reach a point where you realise learning the skill is harder than you thought. This is because you've gained first hand experience about the steps involved in mastery of the subject. This is called the level of Conscious Competence.[3] Unfortunately it's also the point at which people can become overwhelmed and give up. If you're not regularly inserting yourself into new learning situations, you don't appreciate this as a stage to manage through rather than a disaster that makes you stop.

Another key challenge many discover, when they go into business for themselves, is that they're at heart really a practitioner of their skills, rather than a businessperson. Being the practitioner is the part they love. It's also the part they thought they would be doing more of when they committed to this new endeavour. Spending large amounts of time doing necessary activities like administration or promotion, which you don't particularly like or have much aptitude for, can be demoralising.

The key thing to take on board is that you don't have to be perfect or brilliant at everything.

Being effective is about knowing when it makes more sense to stick to what you do well, and where you should utilise the strengths of others. If you're struggling at this point, it's because you don't yet have the mix quite right.

Some approaches

- ✓ **Skills inventory** - Take an inventory of the skills needed to be effective and successful in your chosen field, based on your current understanding (which will change). Group them into three categories: strong skills, weak skills and the skills you don't consider you possess at all. Rank them in order of priority for action.

- ✓ **Skills assessment** - For the skills you either don't have or where you rate yourself poorly, analyse the problem. Is it lack of skill or do you have unrealistic expectations of the time and work involved to master the skill properly?

- ✓ **Learning** - For skills you need to further develop find people or courses that can mentor you, or allocate time to spend improving these skills yourself.

- ✓ **Outsourcing options** - Identify where it makes sense to spend money or barter and where it makes sense to DIY. Your strategy for some skills may be to 'make do' or DIY to a level with a longer-term plan to buy the skills at a later point when you want to scale.

✓ **Role models** - One of the best pieces of advice for advancing in a new field is to find someone who's already doing it well and learn from them. You'll be surprised how much others get a kick out of being asked for help when approached in the right way. Find people online, in your community or in the news. Role models or mentors don't need to be famous or hugely difficult to reach either. They can be people who are accessible and who you consider to be effective in their chosen field.

✓ **Hard** - Realise all endeavours worth doing go through periods of being hard; its just part of the process. Rather than retreating from these challenges, work to overcome them by exercising your resourcefulness muscles. These experiences will provide you with opportunities to be more creative, and to learn that there can be a number of roads to the same outcome. View challenges as opportunities to succeed rather than risks of failure.

Underestimating the Time and Work Effort Involved

We often have unrealistic expectations about how quickly other people will respond to our 'greatness'. Building a business, excelling at what you do or producing great art all take time.

Stories in the media often create the impression that success is easy and happens overnight, because that's a comfortable story. One that bypasses the dreary grind of hard work; the bit where some person worked on their craft in obscurity for a long time often wondering if they would ever make it.

It's easy to bounce around at this point and feel stuck between Denial, Frustration and Depression. You become so overwhelmed by all the things you have to do that you're tempted to sit on the couch all day and do nothing.

I remember talking to a friend years ago who had just embarked on part time study because she wanted to move into a new field. She lived alone, had a full time job and bubbling social life. When I spoke to her she had recently begun her course and was at the point of denial. She resented the course workload and the degree to which it now intruded into her life. She was angry because she thought she could just continue her life as it was and the study would be squeezed in around it. She hadn't yet made the leap of commitment into the realisation that her life was changing. For the next few years study was going to dominate her life outside of work.

We can all fall into this trap of thinking things can both be different and somehow stay the same, they can't. A key element of integration is also displacement. There are things that you may have to stop doing for a while if you are going to succeed in your new direction.

It's also tempting to compare yourself unfavourably with people who have been at their game for a long time and have got much of the juggling worked out. For example, when you're a beginner, aiming to play tennis today better than you played last week is a realistic goal. Aiming to play tennis today better than Roger Federer did last week is not. Use mentors and role models where appropriate, but be realistic about what you can expect from your stage of development.

It's not uncommon for people to find, on the back of a lot of time and hard work that situations can rapidly shift. Suddenly your skill level increases dramatically in some area. Or when you relax, and adopt the mindset that something is going to take longer than you thought, things start to happen. You get a number of job offers or new customers and opportunities or activities begin to accelerate.

I'm reminded of the story of the Devil at the crossroads. This tale, often told about the blues guitarist and singer Robert Johnson, grew around him because early in his career he was not considered to be an especially remarkable musician. He then 'disappeared' for a while and when he returned had transformed into a consummate bluesman. The resulting myth was that he had met the Devil at the crossroads and traded his soul for the ability to really play the blues.

Some things just take time to germinate and can't really be rushed, but the exponential impact of a lot of hard work can create the impression of sudden improvements. The most likely explanation was that it was hard work rather than magic that improved Robert Johnson's playing.

Some approaches

✓ **Recalibrate your expectations about time** - Taking unrealistic time pressures off yourself can be hugely liberating. Time is just an artificial construct, which can apply pressure to situations that previously felt controlled and relaxed. This doesn't mean put your feet up, it means not measuring yourself against a yardstick of what others are doing by adjusting to realistic timeframes. This approach will free you to absorb yourself into the task at hand and concentrate on just getting better. By adopting this mindset, you'll discover things actually don't take that much longer, but you feel so much better about them in the process. Once you start adjusting your expectations you can find yourself much more comfortable with the longer game because you're establishing a solid foundation.

✓ **Letting go and deprioritizing** - To accommodate your new endeavour, you may have to make some fundamental changes to your lifestyle, to ensure you have enough time and energy for the things that matter. The age old problem of Quality vs. Time vs. Price - you can't have all three. So you'll need to deprioritise the Time you spend in some areas of your life to improve the Quality in others.

✓ **Time for major lifestyle changes** - Set yourself up to function optimally. Maybe cut down your alcohol, eat better or get more regular exercise and sleep. You may find when charting your own course that your days are more dynamic, and you need to schedule more downtime than previously. This can sound like rather dull grandmotherly advice but it's more a case of recognising the importance of getting the fundamentals right, if you're using more energy and facing different stressors.

✓ **Multiple streams of work** - Put mechanisms in place to have multiple streams of work on the go, so that if you dry up in one area you'll be able to switch to another. This is also an effective mechanism to manage risk. It gets around the 'all or nothing' high roller strategy, which can lead to frustration and disappointment when projects dry up or become unsuccessful dead ends.

Promotion and Marketing

The extent to which you need to promote and market your work can come as a surprise to many people, which is why it deserves a category all of its own.

One of the great criticisms of the 'follow your passion' industry is that the people involved are too inwardly focused. They're more concerned with what they would like out of the lifestyle equation, than the value they can offer to others. Building a compelling 'What's in it for me?' (WIIFM) proposition is essential if you're really going to connect with an audience and get them to pay you.

Promoting your work can be a massive exercise in frustration; illustrating the reality that, no matter how good you are, it's simply not enough to build it and they will come. You also need to tell them it exists, where it's located and why they should bother.

Unfortunately if you're not a born marketer you may be floundering before you even begin. The truth is, even those born to it get it wrong because marketing and promotion is often more art and science. And it's often easier to promote other people's work than it is your own.

The person who succeeds doesn't necessarily have to be the best, but they are often the person who is the most effective at communicating a message that connects with others.

Promotion and marketing is an area where you would be well advised to seriously improve your skills or hire in professionals. The commodity everyone is clamoring for is people's attention. While we are constantly being bombarded with messages, there are so many more cheap or no cost opportunities to get your message heard.

Some approaches

✓ **It's not about you, it's about them** - Upfront you need to give consideration to the How, What, When, Why and Whom of what you're producing. Without proper analysis and testing in place, you'll be too far advanced before you know if there is even a market for your product. Schedule this key step early.

✓ **Take promotion seriously** - Promotion is not just an afterthought to the main game; it's an integral part, which needs time, money and resources to implement. It can be as much work to promote something, as it was to produce it in the first place.

✓ **Your audience or market isn't everyone** - There's a famous story told by Dita Von Teese when she was first starting out in burlesque. She had a very different look to the other women she worked alongside. While they got small tips from many customers she would get large tips from a select well-heeled few. Remember not everyone is your audience. Scattergun marketing and promotion is a waste of time; search out your particular audience and play to them. The skill rests in locating them and devising a message in the right format, at the right time that they can hear and hopefully take action on. By targeting your approach you can allocate your time and resources most effectively.

- ✓ **Learn what works from others** - Learn what works from others and hire professionals particularly for their experience and connections. You won't have to do too much promotion and marketing yourself before you can appreciate the value a professional can bring.

- ✓ **Always experiment to improve the mix -** Promote in a way that allows you to assess the effectiveness of your approach by using methods that are targeted and measurable. Experiment with different approaches by all means, but don't flog dead horses. If a method or channel doesn't work for you, use another. The many inexpensive online options mean that experimentation doesn't have to be costly.

- ✓ **The power of connections and networks** - Build your networks and connections to help you locate your market/audience and leverage the power of cross-promotional opportunities.

- ✓ **Promotion never ends** - Take every opportunity to promote your work. Promotion isn't a 'set and forget' activity. It's something that never ends until you run out of time, money or decide to stop.

Are You Too Much of a Perfectionist?

Perfectionism is a killer on a number of fronts and there is a fine line between having high standards and being overly perfectionist.

Perfectionism in oneself can be hard to address. Ultimately it's not a road to happiness, but more importantly, it can be the road to inaction. When you're so worried about things not being perfect, you can become so paralysed; you don't produce anything at all. One of the attributes you need to develop is pragmatism. Remember a good idea today beats a great idea tomorrow!

Perfectionism tends to grow out of fear. You're afraid of being judged for not measuring up in some way. Your greatest fear is to be judged by someone like yourself. In a sense you are everyone's worst enemy - Don't be that person!

Some approaches

- ✓ **Broaden your perspective** - Learn from people who have a broader or more relaxed perspective than yourself and see where they focus their energies. There'll be people you know who approach life quite differently to you, but who you consider to be highly effective. Observe how they do and don't 'sweat the small stuff'.

- ✓ **Remember the 80:20 Rule** - Remember the Pareto principle of 80:20. 20% of your effort achieves 80% of the result. Sure it can sometimes be hard to tell what will pay off for you, but you can pretty much guarantee any form of busywork that is not outcome based is not reaping you much benefit. Analyse where you can be the most effective. Start small, but realise you don't have to worry about EVERY LITTLE THING ALL THE TIME. This may feel hard in the beginning and go against the grain of your nature but keep practicing and you will become better at it.

✓ **Prioritise** - You cannot do everything and at the end of each day there will always be things left undone. Accept this fact, prioritise ruthlessly and don't agonise over it.

✓ **Avoid the long 'To Do' list** - The crazily long 'To Do' list is not your friend. If you have a tendency to be easily overwhelmed, the problem may be that you are too detail orientated. You write yourself long exhaustive lists, in an effort to control your life, while the details just consume you. Worrying and writing lists will not help the situation at all. If you have this tendency you may need to helicopter up so that your focus stays on the main game. If you must write lists, keep them short and high level.

✓ **Work on your self-esteem** - Poor self-esteem for whatever reason is often at the heart of perfectionism. It can be challenging when your childhood or past events keep a stranglehold on the present. You may want to seriously consider some professional help with a good therapist or psychologist if you continue struggling to make inroads on your own.

Not Enough of the Doing?

It can be confronting to discover you're really way more in love with the *idea* of something than you are with the cold reality of actually *doing* the work. It's much easier to create an image that impresses some people than it is to actually knuckle down and deliver.

Writing a book is a perfect example. The number of people who fancy themselves as authors is legion. The number who actually get a book written and published is by contrast quite small.

Regardless of how much or how little work you do, if outputs are not materialising, you could be someone who shies away from real action. Unfortunately many activities, especially if they involve planning and talking, *feel* as if you're engaged in real work. Studies have shown that telling people about your goals can create the same 'feel good' in your brain as accomplishing them. Talking effectively becomes a substitute for action in terms of how you feel about yourself.[4]

If something doesn't have a clear outcome it's probably just a 'feel good' activity. "Not that there's anything wrong with that" as Jerry Seinfeld would say, but it becomes a problem if your aim is to progress and you're starting to apportion blame for your inaction to external causes.

Some approaches

✓ **Be clear about your 'Why'** - Revisit your 'Why' so that you have a clear focus for your activities. If an activity doesn't fit in with your 'Why' then de-prioritise it. Ensure you are working on the most important things you have to do. Even if you are overwhelmed and honestly have no idea what you should do next. Take time out to helicopter up and think about your 'Why'. This may help you with the next small step.

✓ **Act and do** - Convert activities into clear action steps and do them.

✓ **Beware of too much planning** - Planning has its place but too much planning and the generation of lists can be a substitute for action. So don't over plan before you start doing. Or keep your planning at a high level from the beginning.

✓ **Break things down into smaller steps** - If something you need to do is intimidating break it down into smaller achievable steps. Make sure you are doing action steps every day even if they are very small. Over time these small steps will add up to a larger body of work that you have essentially 'tricked' yourself into doing. Everything can be broken down into meaningful smaller tasks.

✓ **Make commitments or create deadlines** - There's nothing like setting up a meeting with someone or committing to doing something by a certain date to propel your activities.

✓ **Be outcome focused** - Ask yourself when you are about to do something whether it is an action or a procrastination step. Don't get yourself caught up in busy work where you mistake activity for action

✓ **Don't multitask** - People are reluctant to give up multitasking because it *feels* counterintuitive to accept that it's inefficient. The research suggests you are better doing one thing through to completion and then moving on to the next item, than to have multiple things half done. Lots of incomplete activities hanging over you just contributes to your sense of feeling overwhelmed and stuck.

Chapter 3 - MORE DISTRACTIONS

"Perfectionism is the voice of the oppressor, the enemy of the people. It will keep you cramped and insane your whole life, and it is the main obstacle between you and a shitty first draft. I think perfectionism is based on the obsessive belief that if you run carefully enough, hitting each stepping-stone just right, you won't have to die. The truth is that you will die anyway and that a lot of people who aren't even looking at their feet are going to do a whole lot better than you, and have a lot more fun while they're doing it" – ANNE LAMONT

"If you post a bunch of inspirational quotes every day; your business is probably unprofitable" – UNKNOWN

"A schedule defends from chaos and whim" – ANNIE DILLARD

The previous chapter focused on common challenges that can derail you. This section covers some of the many distractions that can further slow you down by consuming energy and creating a low level sense of drag on your activities.

Discipline, Routines and Scheduling Time Off

When your passion or side hustle becomes your main job, it can be easy for your life to descend into chaos. People often make the mistake of tossing ALL routine aside in an effort to free themselves from 9 to 5 'slavery'. As dull as it may sound, you still need good routines and habits to achieve significant progress, although the routines may now be different. You can't sit there waiting for inspiration to come and for things to happen when you feel like it, because it's not a workable model. You need to establish regular habits and routines that enable the inspiration to be made real.

These regular routines will support your altered state of normal where you may be doing a greater variety of new things. Without the anchor of established routines you're more likely to succumb to feeling overwhelmed and exhausted; or to suffer from decision fatigue.

You also need to schedule in weekends or deliberate downtime when you won't be working. This is one of the issues home workers regularly face. Work and Everything Else bleeds into each other. What starts out, as a glorious opportunity to have more freedom, becomes a form of home detention. Or alternatively, you never seem to be very far away from an electronic device or a screen.

Learning to navigate your way through this freedom paradox is a further expression of Maslow's Hierarchy.

Some approaches

✓ **Develop regular routines and stick to them no matter what!** - One of the keys to setting up good routines is to understand the motivation behind them so they perpetuate themselves effortlessly. Solid routines can organise your life in a way that takes much of the need for decision-making and willpower out of the equation. Applying routines to some of the more mundane aspects of life e.g. what to wear, eat and what time to go to bed etc., will mean you don't tie up so much mental energy in these areas which you can redirect to more worthwhile pursuits.

✓ **Experimentation** - It may take some experimentation to settle on the routines that work best for you. Don't be afraid to try something for while and tweak it to make it better. This approach will build optimised and sustainable habits.

✓ **Work to your natural rhythms** - There's a lot to be said for being a morning person, but if you're not then don't sweat this detail, just arrange your routine accordingly. The main thing is to do the important work of the day when you are at your most alert and productive. Tune in to your natural energy cycles.

✓ **Prioritise creation over consumption** - Tasks where you are creating your own work should take priority over reactive tasks such as responding to your email. Always do your creative work first each day.

✓ **Incremental improvements** - If you are finding it hard to get going then start small with one incremental habit a day. For example, if you want to get up earlier in the morning try the approach of getting up earlier by 1 minute a day. At the end of a month you'll have got up half an hour earlier without much pain. This sustainable approach manages your energy levels. There is nothing like tiredness to make you slip back into bad habits and feeling like not bothering. By making incremental improvement you've tricked yourself into getting up earlier without really trying.

✓ **Recreate away from your main activity** - Set up recreations that take you away from your primary activity. This might be something more physical, artistic, visual, aural, outdoors etc., but you get the picture, something that uses different muscles and senses to what you use everyday. This will develop different aspects of your brain and abilities. You will also discover new things about yourself and your work through cross-fertilizing into different fields.

✓ **Schedule in relaxation time** - Make sure you're structuring in regular downtime to refresh yourself by doing the things you find fun and enjoyable. Even when you have a mountain of work to do, you'll work more efficiently with regular breaks. It's a mistake to think you need to spend all your time working. Like multitasking, working constantly may seem like the most efficient method and your only option, but the research tells a different story.[5] Importantly your brain needs time to goof off and relax so that you're refreshed to focus more fully on the task at hand.

✓ **Develop your powers of concentration** - Clearing your mind of distractions and absorbing yourself completely in the task at hand will lead to far better outcomes. This'll enable you to make the best use of your time, especially in situations where you have less than the ideal conditions, in which to operate – which is probably most of the time! What busy successful people know is that the perfect conditions rarely appear. Increasing your powers of concentration will enable you to make the most of the time available.

✓ **Don't fritter small amounts of time** - It's easy to fall into the trap of thinking that it's not worth starting something because you don't have a huge amount of time available. But it's amazing just now much you can accomplish in small blocks of time if you concentrate and don't multitask. You always have more time than you think. Be more optimistic about what you can accomplish in small parcels of time rather than frittering them away.

✓ **Workspaces** – There's value in creating specific workspaces so that when you are at a particular desk or location you are focused on your work. This approach helps to better compartmentalise your various activities and ensure you are able to switch off by keeping your work and home separate.

✓ **Reduce screen time and the use of alerts** - Be disciplined about the frequency with which you use screens or stay hooked up to other alerts such as messaging and email. These intrusions absorb enormous amounts of mental energy, so that even when you aren't working, you don't feel refreshed because you're still multitasking in a doing or thinking about work mode. Plenty of research is emerging about how our modern way of living is rewiring our brains and inhibiting our ability to think more deeply and maintain our attention over longer periods of time. [6] It can be a source of chronic stress to be always connected and switched 'on'.

Monotony and Boredom

Human beings are wired to seek out novelty and change; it's what got us out of the caves in the first place.

So understandably, you may be puzzled over feelings of monotony in your new situation. It's starting to feel boring like your old job when it was supposed to be fun, right? Yes and no, there are a couple of things going on here.

The first is lack of variety. If you do anything for 40 hours a week, week in week out, it soon becomes monotonous; even lying on the beach, but people can forget this when they decide to turn their side hustle or passion into a full time (or in some cases *more* than full time) business. Too much of the same thing, even when it's a good thing, is monotony by another name.

Secondly research and human experience have shown that people are notoriously bad at working out what will make them happy.[7] There's even a school of thought that argues, it's the Western preoccupation with the search for happiness itself, which is misguided.[8]

The third element is your expectations. EVERYTHING has its shitty moments, days or weeks and it's deluded to expect every minute to be amazing.

Some approaches

- ✓ **Structure in variety** - Build more variety into what you're doing to maintain your interest level and enthusiasm. You either don't have good routines in place yet or have not structured them with enough diversity. For example: do you have the right balance of solo tasks vs. tasks done in collaboration with others? Sitting vs. standing, writing vs. doing, finances vs. creating, talking vs. being on your own. You get the idea.

✓ **Side projects** - One approach is to have a number of projects in the pipeline at different stages. One could be at a point of ideas or discovery, another in implementation and a third in a marketing phase. This approach means you can have multiple streams on the go each requiring different styles of effort from you.

✓ **Find a new hobby** - If what you did previously for a hobby has become your work, then you may need to find yourself a new hobby, something to take your talents into a different field to refresh and energise yourself.

Isolation

Your level of sociability and where you sit on the introvert/extrovert scale impact your need for social interaction. If you're someone who's gone to a regular workplace for years, you may have taken its more sociable aspects for granted. You may also find your lifestyle is now at odds with many of your friends and family, who are working conventional hours so you're no longer free to meet at the same time.

Whatever the reason for your sense of isolation it's important to create a support mechanism through regular contact with people who value you. Work towards a sense of genuine connection, rather than a lot of superficial exchanges. You don't have to say a desperate 'Yes' to every invitation that comes your way, just be willing to try new things and put yourself into situations where you meet new people.

Some approaches

- ✓ **Initiate social contact with others** - Think about how regularly you need social interaction and schedule accordingly. Don't wait to be asked, create events and initiate activities yourself. This will allow you to engage in the types of things that best suit you. Use the numbers method and set up a certain number of social activities each week.

- ✓ **Regular out and about routines** - Set up regular routines that get you out and about. For example a regular coffee at the local coffee shop, work away from home in the local library, join a gym or do volunteer work in an area of interest.

✓ **Review your living arrangements** - Potentially review your living arrangements so that you come into contact with more people as part of your day-to-day activities. This is especially important for single people or those living alone because a predictable level of interaction is not automatically built into your day.

✓ **Go online** - The Internet at its best brings people together with similar interests. There are a number of different groups you can access online via websites and apps like Meetup. Or you can set up your own group to attract other likeminded people. Set yourself up with a Mastermind group for accountability, based on any criteria you name.

✓ **Broaden your network** - Avoid the cultural 'ghetto' even if it feels cosy in there. People doing different things can spark your creativity and help generate new ideas. Think broadly across age groups and interests. Make sure you're spending time with people who are seriously 'doing' rather than just talking about it. Develop a reciprocal social circle so you can genuinely support and raise each other up.

Seasons and SADs

I'm a classic Seasonally Affective Disorder (SADs) person. While we're often misunderstood and dismissed as complainers, I've noticed most people seem much happier and more energetic when the days are longer and the sun is out.

If you're hitting a slump in your motivation and feeling trapped by too much routine, the source of the problem could be the season. Don't underestimate the impact of weather particularly if you are a SADs person. The effect can creep up on you in quite an insidious way.

I have regular video calls with people in other countries so this strikes me frequently. You see a distinct contrast in people's moods when they're in completely different types of clothes and the sun is shining brightly or it's snowing outside.

Some approaches

- ✓ **Be sensitive to SADs** - If you're a SADs person be sensitive to this aspect of yourself and recognise the mood as a regular seasonal phase.

- ✓ **Plan a holiday** - Plan some time in the sun to give yourself a lift. Winter may be a good time of the year to take a short holiday to a place with warmer weather. Even if it is only for a short time, the experience will buoy up your spirits and get you back into a more positive frame of mind.

- ✓ **Be conscious of light sources when indoors** - Be more conscious of natural light sources when indoors so that you position yourself near windows. Also take some time to go outside everyday.

✓ **Change your routine** - If you are falling into a rut, get into a change of routine - shake things up. If travel is not practical, take a holiday in your own city and do some different things.

✓ **Exercise** - If you have scaled back your exercise because the weather is cold, develop a better routine that you can maintain year round.

Are You Searching for the Secret of Happiness or the Meaning of Life

If you've travelled down this road because you want it to provide you with the answers to life's great questions, you may be disappointed.

Your new pursuit will provide you with many things, but it will never compensate if you're starting from a base of need. It will not complete you, love you or make you immune from pain and uncertainty. If you burden it with this level of expectation you will remain dissatisfied.

'Wherever you go; there you are' is true and ultimately you can't run from yourself. If you have a tendency to apply unrealistic expectations or 'if only' scenarios to aspects of your life, this could indicate deeper issues that need addressing before they hit crisis point.

Some approaches

- ✓ **Get to better know thyself** - Now is the perfect time to delve inward and take a break from seeking external validation. This may involve using affirmations, meditation, journaling or other forms of discovery and healing. Make sure you're addressing any possible addictions, past trauma or general patterns that have repeated themselves in your life. These are indicators of unresolved issues.

- ✓ **Ask for feedback** - Ask trusted friends or family for feedback. People who have known you a long time can provide insights into your behaviour and motivations that may surprise you. They can be particularly helpful for identifying your recurring patterns of behaviour.

✓ **Seek help** - Get external assistance to mine through this stuff in a supported way with a discrete professional who is outside your immediate circle of family and friends. While both scary and confronting to contemplate, this approach can really accelerate your understanding of yourself and move you forward.

Fear of Success

Fear of success can be a surprising combination of fears: pressure, scrutiny, change or even just the speed at which things are moving in your world. It's easy to self-sabotage at this point by not doing what needs to be done, then blaming external reasons for your derailment.

People don't often tell you about the problems of success. One of the worst can be discovering you have even less time and more commitments than you had before. Drowning in a sea of pressure you neither expected nor can cope with is frightening. Your definition of success may even undergo an overhaul at this point.

You either need a respite or some form of assistance to cope with these changes.

Some approaches

- ✓ **Remember you're in a state of transition** - Highly successful people go through differing stages when adjusting to their levels of success. They didn't have all the answers either in the beginning, so ease up on yourself.

- ✓ **Don't go it alone** - Reach out and ask for the support and the advice you need.

- ✓ **Identify further skill gaps** - These may be things like handling the media, time management, public speaking, relaxation or even the tricks of how to look into a camera and appear good in photos. You may encounter many new situations with unanticipated problems that you could resolve with access to the right skills and training. Make your life easier by availing yourself of the best information and teachers to improve your confidence.

✓ **Practice makes perfect** - The more you practice your new skills the better and more polished you will become, so seize opportunities to practice often and it will get easier.

✓ **Beware of excuses** - When you find yourself making excuses and externalising blame it's a sign you're operating from a fear response. Be honest with yourself about your fears and put mechanisms in place to contain them, rather than allowing them to continually sabotage you.

✓ **Understand what success means to you** - So that you are clear about the tradeoffs you're willing to make; there will always be tradeoffs.

Chapter 4 - OVERARCHING IDEAS

"The strongest of all warriors are these two — Time and Patience" - LEO TOLSTOY, *War and Peace*

"Whatever it takes to finish things, finish. You will learn more from a glorious failure than you ever will learn from something you never finished" - NEIL GAIMAN

"….When you want something, all the universe conspires in helping you to achieve it" - PAUL COELHO

There are a number of concepts or principles that come up time and again because they effectively underpin much else. These are the ideas that are always worth revisiting because if you apply them consistently to most situations you'll experience results.

The Importance of Persistence

Persistence distinguishes people who succeed from people who don't. The person, who stays the course, to emerge as the 'last person standing', is often the one who gets the prize. The determination to persist can be a greater indicator of success than talent.

People are often so close to their goals when they give up. When you're feeling dejected the best advice is to keep going. Keep moving forward even if it's to the smallest degree:

- ✓ If you are writing a novel write just one more word.

- ✓ If you are starting up a business send just one more email

✓ If you don't know what to do next send one Tweet asking for advice

And the next day, do the same all over again and you will incrementally move forward. Even if you can't see the whole path or even if you don't know whether there even is a path. Just keep moving forward and the next logical steps in the plan will reveal itself. The main thing is to not give up.

Another way of looking at this is to commit to the choice you've made and make it the right choice for you. Back yourself and prove you're right.

Don't let setbacks or other obstacles get in your way; use them to your advantage.

Confidence and Commitment

When you're in new situations be confident that you can do well. The magic of confidence is that you make a decision to rely on yourself. While it can appear to be a version of the old 'fake it till you make it' veneer, it's really about developing and projecting the rock solid self belief that you can do this.

Tim Grahl in the *Book launch blueprint* says the fundamental first step to launching a successful book is to absolutely believe in what you are doing. 'You have to believe in the deepest part of your soul, that it is a *good thing for readers* to buy and read your book'. This level of conviction applies to everything.

Believe in what you are doing. Full commitment is the bedrock on which you can progress. It will transcend the self-doubt, half-heartedness and fear that create so much of your resistance.

Accountability

Accountability - *an obligation or willingness to accept responsibility or to account for one's actions.*

The term accountability is often applied to public officials, especially in the context of owning up to your mistakes. One of the challenges faced by people who've come out of a more conventional way of life, is they struggle to accept the broader accountability that comes from leading a more independent or creative path. In many respects, this can be the point at which you become fully an adult for the first time.

Accountability means taking responsibility for ALL aspects of your life:

- ✓ Health
- ✓ Fitness
- ✓ Diet and nutrition
- ✓ Finance
- ✓ Marketing and promotion
- ✓ Public speaking
- ✓ Assertiveness
- ✓ Networking
- ✓ Writing
- ✓ Relaxation
- ✓ Time management
- ✓ Curiosity

- ✓ Growth
- ✓ Resilience
- ✓ Critical thinking
- ✓ Relationships

When the buck stops completely with you it can be very scary. Fortunately in the age of online, it's now easier than ever to access the resources you need to strengthen your less developed abilities.

Create yourself and be confident that the best approach for you is the one that works for you.

Learning to Say 'No' Way More Often

If you're the sort of person who's been socialised to please or someone who just has a general Fear of Missing Out (FOMO). Then saying 'No' to other people can feel absolutely loaded, as if you're twisting yourself out of shape.

When the important things that matter to you remain undone and time gets away, that's about the opportunity cost of saying 'No' to yourself because you have said 'Yes' to other people. Often we don't make this decision consciously. Learning to say 'No' to others is about making a commitment to you; charting your life rather than just reacting to circumstances.

Derek Sivers in his great book *Anything you want* talks about the clarifying concept of 'HELL YEAH! or no'. What he basically argues is that when you're weighing up whether to say 'Yes' or 'No' to something what you should really be considering is whether it's a 'HELL YEAH' or 'No". In other words, if your first reaction isn't 'Hell yeah, I so want to do this!' then it's clearly a 'No'.

Be Kind to Yourself

Be kind to yourself through this process because you're not a machine and are more fragile than you think. Nurture yourself as you would a small child who you love dearly and want only the best for in the world. Regularly make time for the things you enjoy and make sure you offer them to yourself as treats.

Be conscious of your emotional responses to situations and people because these are important barometers of how you're travelling. Don't be tempted to neglect and beat up yourself, because that's just a waste of time. Settle in and pace yourself for the long haul.

Learn to navigate through a more dynamic reality where you anticipate ups and downs. When you accept that at least some obstacles are inevitable, you can put mechanisms in place to overcome them, rather than feeling overwhelmed when situations don't go according to plan. Give yourself the level of support you would like to receive from others.

Meditation

Meditation is a beneficial practice I can't recommend enough. Many high achieving people incorporate some form of meditation into their daily routine.

The practice of mediation centers you and brings you back to yourself. It provides clarity and a way to manage stress and anxiety. Most importantly, it provides you with the regular experience of being fully conscious of what real relaxation feels like. You then can return to this state more easily when you are in the midst of stressful situations.

When I was going through a period of significant change in my life a couple of years ago. I just felt this overwhelming need to retreat into myself and meditate. The pull was incredibly strong. I couldn't even tell you where it came from, just that I needed to do it. I started meditating daily for five minutes, and slowly increased to 15 minutes per day, which I now do regularly each morning.

Start a regular habit of meditation and see what you experience for yourself.

Reach the Finish Line

People ask me how I wrote my first book and I tell them it was straightforward: You start; you keep going and then you finish. Notice I didn't say it was *easy* just that it was straightforward, which is a very important distinction.

We all have vast 'To do' lists and many unfinished projects because while starting can be easy and fun, finishing things is hard work. The last few percent as you polish and bring something through to completion is often the place where you can potentially put in the greatest amount of effort. No amount of thinking about it, talking or being in the proximity of the finish line is a substitute for the actual doing. This is particularly important if you have multiple streams of activity on the go. You must structure them in such a way that you're working towards completion. If nothing else, it can be a massive mental drain having too many unfinished projects, because it generates a sense of feeling overwhelmed without the achievement.

It's also important to draw the distinction between completing something worthwhile versus abandoning a poor idea and it can be hard to tell the difference. The singer songwriter Leonard Cohen puts this in another way when he says, "the cutting of the gem has to be finished before you can see whether it shines". It's sometimes not till you get to the finish line that you fully understand the real value of what you've created.

Arrive at Integration

Revisiting the *Change Curve* diagram in Chapter 1, you'll recall that the last important stage of moving through any type of change is Integration.

This is where you take the best of what you've experienced, heard and seen and blend them together into the most effective approach for you.

This integration process continues throughout your life as you're constantly exposed to new things and assessing where they fit into the grand scheme of your whole of life experience.

The ability to integrate your experiences well, to toss out and replace or to shuffle things around, is ultimately the key to how effective are you in charting your life forward.

In summary

Here's a graphic to keep upfront and center to remind you ☺

HOW TO BECOME UNSTUCK

By Chloe Hill from the new book " Stuck?: When Your Dream Becomes Work"

Have a clear purpose

State your pupose to yourself every day to maintain focus

Manage your fear

Train to become more comfortable with fear, there is no antidote but desensitisation

Just say 'no'

Say 'yes' to the right things. Prioritise your time by saying 'no' more often

Curb your perfectionism

Remember a good idea today beats a great idea tomorrow! Perfectionism is the road to inaction and excuses

Develop Discipline

Develop effective habits and routines - even schedule for rewards and time out. Move away from chaos

Finish things

Starting is easy, but it's finishing something that makes all the difference. When you aim to complete things you'll actually achieve and learn so much

Take action

Don't overthink, act. Take 'baby steps' and break the big things down into the smallest action steps - then do them!

Persist

Keep going no matter what. Even if you're moving slowly, you're still moving

Integrate what you learn

Consider past, present and future. Don't ditch what works, make it better. Integrate the new in with the old. This process is lifelong

And lastly

Could it be time to ask the hard questions?

Initially I hesitated including this section in the book at all. I didn't want to be negative, but I did want to offer practical wisdom.

You're at a point now where you've learned a hell of a lot about yourself as you've spent time pursuing your dream, but what kind of adventure has it been? Some adventures take us permanently to new places, while others do more to teach us the value of what we already have and where we've come from.

Through first hand experience you may now have a changed perspective. Potentially you've realised what you have is a good side hustle and that's where it should stay. It adds an important dimension to your life, but is never realistically going to be your main income stream. You're now more aware of the sacrifices and hard work involved. Sacrifices you may not be willing to make when it comes to the crunch. Maybe it's time to return home to Kansas 'Dorothy' a wiser and different person, even if only temporarily to regroup for a while.

The main thing to realise is that whatever you decide at this point is perfectly fine. This is not about failure or giving up; it's about gaining wisdom and acting on what would be best for *you*. If you're unhappy or twisted out of shape in some way that's not good, even if you're running with the 'cool' alternative kids. Don't feel pressured by what other people may think if you decide something is not for you.

It can be a fine line between pragmatism and settling, but people have been doing it for centuries. It's the essence of being an adult as opposed to a self-indulgent child. One of the key learnings you'll have gained at this point is that every situation is a mixed bag of good and bad, no matter how fantastic it may appear from the outside.

You don't know what lies in the future and where all the knowledge and experience you've gained in the pursuit of new paths will lead you. While the present moment can feel like the end of something, you still have further to go and more unknown experiences ahead. View the present as nothing more than a continuation of the path you've begun towards the getting of wisdom.

One of life's confronting secrets is that we're not all created equal. People's talents and abilities follow a normal distribution like everything else. There are a lot fewer people at the extremes of the hopeless and super gifted, than there are in the middle average. Scott Adams the creator of Dilbert expressed the opinion that 'passion feels very democratic. It's the people's talent, available to all'. [9] People who are successful often want to maintain some humility about their success. So they don't tell the world 'they succeeded because [they're] far smarter than the average person'. Instead they say they've simply followed their 'passion'. The truth is they succeeded through extraordinary talent and commitment to hard work. Steve Jobs or Mark Zuckerberg aren't like everyone else, but most of us are.

About the Author

I left the corporate world to pursue a life in writing.

I began noticing in my own journey along the 'road less travelled' that there seemed to be way more material inspiring you to *start*, than there was about helping you to *keep going* when the situation got difficult.

Anyone can be a problem identifier and critic, but it's much harder to give people practical approaches to solving their problems rather than mere platitudes and 'inspiration'.

Whilst coming to grips with my own new experiences and emotions, I wanted to grab those feelings and articulate them. I wanted to dig myself out of my own 'stuck' crisis while at the same time help others.

I hope I've been able to achieve that aim, and you've found at least some, parts of the book useful in getting yourself unstuck!

❀ ❀ ❀

Chloe Hill is also the author of *Why the red face: dealing with rosacea 101* available in paperback and online. She can be contacted via her publisher at info@stivesmedia.com.au

Author Thanks

Book writing can be a lonely pursuit that takes you away, for significant periods, from the people and things that matter most. Special thanks are owed to those who've supported and encouraged me throughout the writing of this book.

My husband Alan, who is endlessly supportive, and has the patience just to listen. He created my beautiful graphics and continues to astound me with his ability to turn his talent to just about anything.

Julie for being my special second reader, always there with her encouragement and support. Julie is astounding for being a zero procrastinator – she always gets straight on to to everything!

Erika and Melissa for being my early readers, who were there at the beginning when this book was just an idea. Melissa's attention to visual detail on my drafts was invaluable.

Jean and Suzanne who always unwaveringly believed and supported me, your endless encouragement always meant a great deal!

Jane, for being available to talk all things authors and writing together and who inspires with her hard work and commitment to her own writing.

Further References

Books

Adams, Scott *How to fail at almost everything and still win big: Kind of the story of my life* Penguin 2013
By the creator of *Dilbert* who has written one of the most useful autobiographical/self-help books on the market (if that is it's own sub genre?) Very honest about success from someone who has wildly succeeded.

Altucher, James *Choose yourself* CreateSpace Independent Publishing Platform, 2013
Great source of information for people wanting to strike out in a more independent or autonomous life direction. A really smart guy!

Altucher, James & Altucher, Claudia Azula *The Power of no: because one little word can bring health, abundance and happiness* Hay House Inc., 2014
Strongly articulates the case for saying 'No'.

Bennett, Michael & Sarah *F*uck feelings: One shrink's practical advice for managing all life's impossible problems* Simon & Schuster 2015
Goes refreshingly against the grain and provides tough love and practical wisdom.

Carr, Nicholas *The Shallows: What the Internet is doing to our brain* W.W. Norton and Company 2010
Game changer of a book that makes you think about the Darwinian adaptations our brain is making in response to an increasingly online world.

Ferriss Tim *The 4-hour workweek: escape 9-5, live anywhere, and join the new rich* Harmony 2009
Probably the father of the modern 'live your passion' industry.

Gilbert, Daniel *Stumbling on happiness* Vintage 2007
Very popular book which exploded the happiness myth and posed a compelling counter argument to our propensity to be dissatisfied and always seeking.

Grahl, Tim *Book launch blueprint: the step-by-step guide to launching a bestseller* Common Insights, 2015
Valuable book in an age of social media marketing which describes how staying simple is often the best way to succeed.

Holiday, Ryan *The Obstacle is the way: the timeless way of turning trials into triumph* Portfolio, 2014
Powerful book written by the Ex-Marketing Director of American Apparel about how obstacles and difficulties are the whole point. How you can become more resilient through expecting and embracing challenges rather than avoiding them.

Lamont, Anne Bird by bird: some instructions on writing and life Anchor, 1995
A frequently referenced and thoughtful book about how to live and tackle tasks that seem at first overwhelming.

Lander, Christian *Stuff white people like: a definitive guide to the unique taste of millions* Random House, 2008
A funny and insightful take on mass consumer marketing in the modern age. Defining what it means to belong to our individual tribes.

Poulson, Ingrid *Rise* Macmillan Australia, 2008
An extraordinary book written by a woman who has been through significant tragedy and discovered that her world didn't end and that she was far more resilient than she realised. Ingrid then went on to analyse why this was the case and what this says about us as human beings.

Sivers, Derek *Anything you want: 40 lessons for a new kind of entrepreneur* Portfolio, 2015
By the former owner and creator of the online music store CD Baby. Provides a distillation of his wisdom about what it takes you really succeed as an independent entrepreneur. You will always get left field advice from this guy.

Websites

Get a great introduction to the concept of 'Rejection Therapy'. Jia Jiang runs through the surprising results of his '100 days of rejection' challenge. Fearbuster.com

Website, with it's own app, which enables you to make contact with all sorts of special interest groups happening all over the world - or to start your own. Meetup.com

Michael Hyatt is the former Chairman and CEO of Thomas Nelson Publishers. He's now an author, blogger and speaker. Always worth a look, his information is practical and slanted towards people operating effectively in a business context Michaelhyatt.com

Videos

Surprising lessons from 100 days of rejection, Jia Jiang at TEDx Austin, February 19, 2013 https://youtu.be/ZFWyseydTkQ, Retrieved August 14 2016.

How to stop screwing yourself over, Mel Robbins at TEDx San Francisco, Uploaded June 11, 2011 http://tedxtalks.ted.com/video/How-To-Stop-Screwing-Yourself-O, Retrieved August 27 2016.

Keep your goals to yourself, Derek Sivers at TEDGlobal July 2010 https://www.ted.com/talks/derek_sivers_keep_your_goals_to_yourself?language=en, Retrieved August 20 2016.

About the Publisher

St Ives Media is a publishing house based in Melbourne, Australia. Check out our range of titles at stivesmedia.com.au

If you would like further information please contact us on info@stivesmedia.com.au

Notes

---

[1] Surprising lessons from 100 days of rejection, Jia Jiang at TEDx Austin, February 19, 2013 https://youtu.be/ZFWyseydTkQ, Retrieved August 14 2016.

[2] How to stop screwing yourself over, Mel Robbins at TEDx San Francisco, Uploaded June 11, 2011 http://tedxtalks.ted.com/video/How-To-Stop-Screwing-Yourself-O, Retrieved August 27 2016.

[3] 'Learning a new skill is easier said than done' by Linda Adams 2016, gordontraining.com Retrieved August 20 2016.

[4] Keep your goals to yourself, Derek Sivers at TEDGlobal July 2010 https://www.ted.com/talks/derek_sivers_keep_your_goals_to_yourself?language=en, Retrieved August 20 2016.

[5] 'Multitasking: switching costs' American Psychological Association, March 20 2006, http://www.apa.org/research/action/multitask.aspx Retrieved August 20 2016.

[6] Carr, Nicholas *The Shallows: What the Internet is doing to our brain* W.W. Norton and Company 2010.

[7] Gilbert, Daniel *Stumbling on happiness* Vintage 2007.

[8] Bennett, Michael & Sarah *F*uck feelings: One shrink's practical advice for managing all life's impossible problems* Simon & Schuster 2015.

[9] Adams, Scott *How to fail at almost everything and still win big: Kind of the story of my life* Penguin 2013.